EARTH'S TREASURES
DIAMONDS

CHRISTINE PETERSEN

ABDO Publishing Company

Published by ABDO Publishing Company, PO Box 398166, Minneapolis, MN 55439.
Copyright © 2014 by Abdo Consulting Group, Inc. International copyrights reserved in all
countries. No part of this book may be reproduced in any form without written permission from the
publisher. The Checkerboard Library™ is a trademark and logo of ABDO Publishing Company.

Printed in the United States of America, North Mankato, Minnesota.
052013
092013

 PRINTED ON RECYCLED PAPER

Cover Photo: iStockphoto
Interior Photos: Alamy pp. 5, 9, 17, 21; AP Images pp. 17, 23, 27; Corbis pp. 11, 13, 20, 26;
    Getty Images pp. 4, 5, 12, 15, 22; iStockphoto pp. 1, 6, 10, 14–15, 19, 21, 24–25, 29;
    Science Source pp. 6–7; Superstock p. 28; Thinkstock pp. 18, 24–25, 29

Editors: Rochelle Baltzer, Megan M. Gunderson
Art Direction: Neil Klinepier

Library of Congress Control Number: 2013932667

Cataloging-in-Publication Data

Petersen, Christine.
 Diamonds / Christine Petersen.
  p. cm. -- (Earth's treasures)
ISBN 978-1-61783-870-5
Includes bibliographical references and index.
1. Diamonds--Juvenile literature. 2. Precious stones--Juvenile literature. 3. Gems--Juvenile
literature. I. Title.
553.8--dc23

2013932667

CONTENTS

KING EDWARD'S GIFT

The Cullinan diamond was discovered on January 25, 1905. It weighed 1 1/3 pounds (0.6 kg).

On November 9, 1907, King Edward VII of Great Britain turned 66 years old. In honor of his birthday, a present was delivered from South Africa. It was a stone about the size of his fist. When he first saw it, the king was not impressed. He thought it looked like a plain chunk of glass. Why would the people of South Africa give King Edward such a gift?

The mystery was soon solved. This was the Cullinan diamond! It was three times as large as any diamond ever found. The people of South Africa had sent him their greatest treasure.

Most diamonds used in fine jewelry weigh just one carat or less. That's 200 milligrams, or about the

4

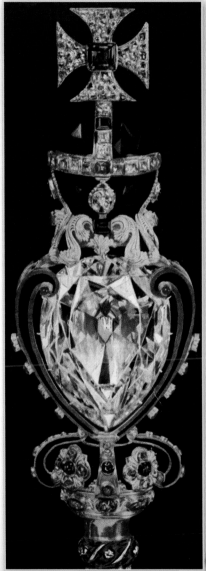

weight of a paper clip. The Cullinan was massive at 3,106 carats!

King Edward sent the diamond to gem cutters, who carved it to make many beautiful jewels. The largest piece is now mounted in the English **scepter**. The second-largest piece is in the Imperial State Crown used by Edward's descendant Queen Elizabeth II.

It took eight months to cut the Cullinan into 9 large stones and more than 100 smaller pieces.

WHAT IS DIAMOND?

Ancient people knew how to shape metal and stone. They molded tools, carved decorations, and crafted jewelry. But diamond was like no other material they had found. It is stronger than any other natural substance on Earth.

Where did this powerful substance come from? Ancient Greeks suggested that diamonds were the tears of the gods. Romans had another idea. They believed diamonds must be broken pieces of stars that had fallen to Earth.

Modern scientists have confirmed that diamond is a mineral. About 3,000 different minerals occur on Earth. Each is **unique**, but they share certain properties. Minerals are usually inorganic. This means they were made in

The atoms in a diamond are so close together they actually slow down light. That's what makes diamonds so sparkly!

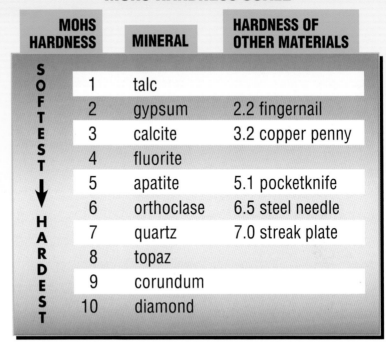

MOHS HARDNESS SCALE

MOHS HARDNESS		MINERAL	HARDNESS OF OTHER MATERIALS
S O F T E S T ↓ **H A R D E S T**	1	talc	
	2	gypsum	2.2 fingernail
	3	calcite	3.2 copper penny
	4	fluorite	
	5	apatite	5.1 pocketknife
	6	orthoclase	6.5 steel needle
	7	quartz	7.0 streak plate
	8	topaz	
	9	corundum	
	10	diamond	

the earth rather than by living things. Minerals are generally solid rather than liquid or gaseous.

Most minerals are made of at least two chemical elements. Yet diamond is different. It contains only carbon. Microscopic atoms are the building blocks of elements. In minerals, atoms link together in repeating patterns to form three-dimensional crystals. Diamond gets its strength from the way its atoms link together.

WELCOME TO KIMBERLEY

Throughout history, people had found diamonds in the gravel of riverbeds. Then, a discovery in South Africa changed everything. A man found diamonds on a hill, rather than near a river.

The news spread quickly. Thousands of people arrived with shovels and pans, hoping to get rich. The Kimberley mine was founded in 1871, and the mining town now called Kimberley was born.

Mining at Kimberley began on a small hill that stood alone. Miners dug until the hill disappeared. Then they dug deeper and deeper, making a pit in the ground.

At first they found diamonds in a layer of yellow, gravelly soil. These were easy to remove. Below this was a layer of blue slate. This stone had to be broken apart. Diamonds were sorted from the soil and rubble.

By 1914, miners had taken all the diamonds they could find at Kimberley. The total was more than 14.5 million carats. To find the diamonds, 24.8 million tons (22.5 million t) of earth had been moved. Today this "Big Hole" is a popular tourist site. It covers an area larger than 30 football fields. And it is more than 700 feet (210 m) deep!

Today, the observation deck at the Big Hole features a space that is just over 30 by 30 feet (9 by 9 m). This was the size of an individual mining claim. From there, visitors can look down on the largest crater in the world to be dug by hand.

9

FROM THE DEEP

All the diamonds at Kimberley were found in a special type of igneous rock. The rock is called kimberlite to honor the place it was discovered. The kimberlite formed a narrow pipe that cut up through other layers of rock. Miners never reached the bottom of this pipe!

Why are diamonds found in kimberlite pipes? It all starts in Earth's mantle, which is below the crust. In the mantle is **magma**. Scientists believe diamonds formed there more than 2 to 3 billion years ago.

Then millions of years ago, magma exploded up into the crust. It carried the diamonds up toward the surface. When

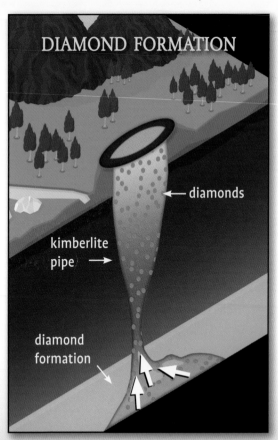

DIAMOND FORMATION

diamonds

kimberlite pipe →

diamond formation

One of the world's largest diamond mines is in Mirny, Russia. It is 1,722 feet (525 m) deep! Today, some people have proposed turning the giant hole into a domed city with homes and even trees.

it cooled, a long **cylinder** or cone of igneous rock remained. Kimberlite formations have since been found on almost every continent. And today, diamonds are mined everywhere except Europe and Antarctica.

Lamproite is another igneous rock that sometimes contains diamonds. The world's largest lamproite mine is in Argyle, Australia.

MINING DIAMONDS

Open-pit mining is used to find diamonds trapped in igneous rock. Explosives loosen the rock. Then, excavators dig up the rocks and load them onto trucks.

Underground mining is another way to find diamonds. Miners use tunnels to find diamonds deeper below the surface.

Not all diamonds are found deep underground. Rain, ice, and wind

In open-pit mining, enormous machines move tons of rock to find tiny diamonds.

cause rock to crack and crumble. Over time, diamonds are released unharmed. They tumble downhill and settle in streambeds. These are called **alluvial** diamond deposits. Miners scoop river rocks and sand into pans. They wash and sort this material to find the diamonds.

Conflict Diamonds

Today, the diamond industry and diamond consumers are working hard to avoid blood diamonds, or conflict diamonds. Blood diamonds are those sold to benefit rebel groups in certain countries.

The profits are often used to buy things such as weapons. At the same time, diamond miners may suffer while leaders make money.

The Kimberley Process was established in 2003. The goal is to stop the trade of blood diamonds and ensure diamonds for sale are conflict free.

In some areas, individuals or communities seek diamonds using basic equipment. This is called artisanal mining.

Countless diamonds have traveled even farther. They have tumbled downstream all the way to the sea. Ships are sent out to suck up these deposits with powerful vacuum hoses. Gravel is sorted on the ship or brought back to shore.

After rock is collected, diamonds must be separated from it. First, the rock is crushed. Then, the broken rock is spun rapidly in water. Large, heavy diamonds fall to the bottom. Anything that sinks is passed through an X-ray machine. Diamonds **fluoresce**, or shine, when X-rayed. So, they are easy to collect.

Any leftover material is dropped onto a grease table. The table shakes as water flows across it and carries away bits of rock. The diamonds stick to the grease table. So, workers can pick them out.

Diamond mining began 2,000 years ago. Today, the Argyle mine in Australia

can process 12 million tons (11 million t) of **ore** each year. That may seem like a lot! But miners may have to move more than a ton of rock to find just one carat of diamonds.

Special ships collect diamonds from offshore deposits.

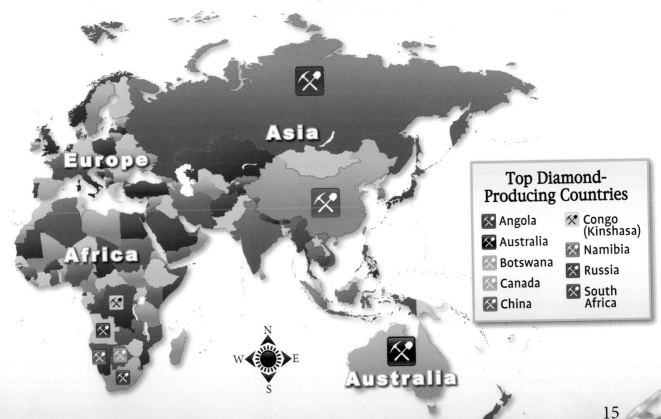

Asia

Europe

Africa

Australia

Top Diamond-Producing Countries

Angola	Congo (Kinshasa)
Australia	Namibia
Botswana	Russia
Canada	South Africa
China	

MINER FOR A DAY

Diamonds have been found in at least 35 countries. But you don't have to travel the world to find them. Crater of Diamonds State Park in Arkansas sits atop a funnel-shaped crater that is 100 million years old. Over time, the surface layers of this rock have **weathered**. So, diamonds are found in the soil.

Diamonds are typically eight-sided. They look like two little pyramids with the bases put together. The crystals may also look like rounded, glassy pebbles.

Most diamonds at Crater of Diamonds State Park are colorless, yellow, or brown. Color occurs when tiny amounts of other elements take the place of carbon atoms in the crystal.

Become a Rock Hound!

WOULD YOU LIKE TO START YOUR OWN COLLECTION OF GEMS AND MINERALS? BECOME A ROCK HOUND!

To get started, locate an area likely to have the treasures you seek. Before you head out, be sure it is legal and you have permission to collect specimens from your search area. Then, gather the tools and safety gear you'll need. Don't forget to bring an adult!

Label your treasures with the date and location you found them. Many rock hounds set a goal for their collections. For example, they might gather samples of all the minerals found in their state or province.

Finally, always leave the land in better shape than you found it. Respecting the environment helps preserve it for future rock hounds and the rest of your community.

WHAT WILL YOU NEED?
map
compass
magnifying glass
hard hat or bicycle helmet
safety goggles
sunscreen
bucket
shovel
rock hammer
pan or screen box
containers for your finds

Diamond hunting is fun but dirty work!

17

KINDS OF CARBON

Diamonds are much older than the rocks in which they are found. These crystals formed billions of years ago more than 100 miles (160 km) below Earth's surface. They surfaced millions of years later during violent volcanic explosions that left behind kimberlite or lamproite.

Deep down in Earth's mantle, pressure can be 50,000 times greater than on the surface. And, it can be as hot as 2,200 degrees Fahrenheit (1,200°C). These conditions squeeze carbon atoms together to create hard, durable diamonds.

Graphite is another mineral made of carbon. But, it forms under less pressure and less heat. So, its atoms are arranged

Diamond and graphite are both forms of carbon. The way carbon atoms are arranged gives diamond and graphite the special properties that make them so different!

differently from diamond. Carbon atoms in graphite form thin sheets. It takes only a little pressure to separate them. Your pencil lead is made with graphite. As you write, graphite sheets are pushed onto the paper.

Carbon can also form particles without a regular crystal structure. These types of carbon include charcoal, which is used as fuel.

Fullerenes are another type of carbon. Even numbers of carbon atoms combine to create hollow shapes. Fullerenes can be used in medicine and electronics.

Cutting Diamonds

Several thousand minerals occur on Earth. But fewer than 200 are considered gemstones. Gems are special because they are uncommon. They are also durable enough to survive years of wear and handling.

Perhaps the most important quality of gems is their beauty. While many common minerals are colorful, gems have extraordinary sparkle and shine. They can be cut or polished for use in jewelry and other decorative objects.

An expert who cuts gems is a called a lapidary. A diamond cutter is someone who **specializes** in diamonds. It takes years of training to do this job well.

Today, experts use saws coated with diamond dust to cut diamonds.

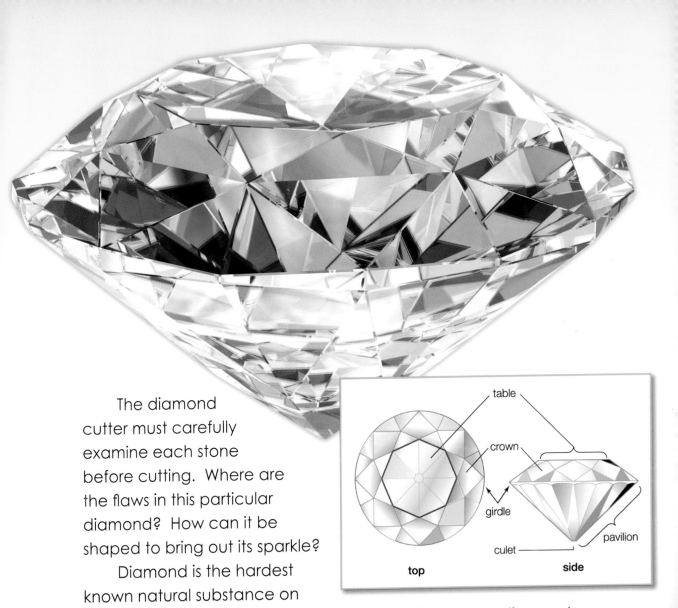

The diamond cutter must carefully examine each stone before cutting. Where are the flaws in this particular diamond? How can it be shaped to bring out its sparkle?

Diamond is the hardest known natural substance on Earth. Ancient people knew no way to cut it! Modern diamond cutters use saws coated with diamond dust or **lasers** in their work.

21

THE FOUR CS

Diamonds can be colorless, yellow, brown, black, blue, green, pink, and purple. Red is the rarest diamond color.

No two diamonds are alike, even after diamond cutters fashion them into familiar shapes. So, experts use four qualities to compare them. These are color, clarity, cut, and carat. Higher scores in each category increase the value of a diamond.

Diamonds occur in almost every imaginable color. That can be good or bad. The best diamonds are colorless or show an intense, solid color throughout. Colored diamonds are called "fancy."

Clarity refers to flaws in a diamond. These affect its brilliance, because they change how light passes through the diamond. Light makes the best diamonds flicker and wink like fire.

Other elements besides carbon cause diamonds to be different colors. The Hope Diamond is blue because of the element boron.

23

round   marquise   pear

trillion   heart   princess

A diamond cutter makes average diamonds more beautiful by cutting them well. He or she considers where the flaws are before cutting. Then **facets** are cut in a geometric pattern over the surface. Facets allow light to enter from many angles.

Find Your Birthstone!

January	February	March	April	May	June
garnet	amethyst	aquamarine	diamond	emerald	pearl

oval

emerald

There are numerous common diamond cuts. Each gem is cut to be as beautiful as possible!

A large diamond is more valuable than two smaller diamonds totaling the same weight. So, the amount of carats is important to a diamond's value. A diamond cutter must cut a diamond well without making it too small.

Many people think of a fifth quality when buying diamonds. They want the gems to be mined **conscientiously**. Conscientious mining companies pay fair wages to their workers. They do not mine in countries that use diamonds to pay for war. In this way, many people work to avoid purchasing conflict diamonds.

July	August	September	October	November	December
ruby	peridot	sapphire	opal	topaz	turquoise

NO WASTE

Diamond scalpels are used in eye surgery.

Most diamonds are too small or imperfect to be cut for jewelry. These crystals do not go to waste! They may not be gems, but they are still useful.

Lapidaries use industrial diamonds to cut gems. Diamond saws are also used to cut out large, metal aircraft parts. This ensures accurate cuts so the edges fit together smoothly. Massive diamond-coated saws carve stone blocks used for countertops. And diamond paste can be used to polish eyeglass lenses. It is like fine sandpaper.

Have you been to the dentist lately? The drill used to smooth your filling may have been tipped with diamond. Some surgical blades also are made from industrial diamonds. These scalpels make tiny cuts with perfect edges. Diamond scalpels are ideal for eye surgery and plastic surgery of the skin.

Giant diamond saws cut granite for monuments and other uses.

27

DIAMOND'S FUTURE

Scientists have long wondered whether they could make diamonds in a laboratory. Companies in Sweden and the United States finally succeeded in the 1950s. To make **synthetic** diamonds, machines create high pressures and temperatures like those in Earth's mantle. This turns graphite into diamond.

Synthetic diamonds have the same chemical structure as natural diamonds. In 2011, almost 59 million carats of diamonds were used by American industries. Nearly 99 percent were synthetic!

Synthetic diamonds can now be grown in just a few days. They are clear and flawless. Only an expert can tell whether your diamond jewelry is human-made. Cubic zirconia is another

Today, more than 15 countries can produce synthetic diamonds.

28

synthetic option. It is made from the elements zirconium and oxygen instead of carbon. Like diamond, it is colorless, hard, and brilliant. People enjoy its sparkle and low price.

Diamonds have been admired for thousands of years. Industries depend on them. Individuals treasure them. These amazing minerals improve our lives in countless ways.

Many people appreciate that cubic zirconia (left) looks much like diamond (below).

GLOSSARY

alluvial - relating to sand, dirt, and rock left by flowing water.

conscientious (kahnt-shee-EHNT-shuhs) - concerned with doing something correctly.

cylinder - a solid bounded by two parallel circles and a curved surface. A soda can is an example of a cylinder.

facet - a small flat surface on a gem.

fluoresce (flu-REHS) - to give off visible light when exposed to a different type of radiation, such as ultraviolet light.

laser - a device that creates a narrow beam of light.

magma - melted rock beneath Earth's surface.

ore - a mineral containing something valuable, such as metal, which is mined.

scepter - a staff held by a ruler as a symbol of authority.

specialize - to pursue one branch of study, called a speciality.

synthetic - something that is human-made by a chemical process.

unique - being the only one of its kind.

weather - to break down rock in its original position at or near Earth's surface.

Saying It

carat - KEHR-uht
igneous - IHG-nee-uhs
kimberlite - KIHM-buhr-lite
lapidary - LA-puh-dehr-ee

Web Sites

To learn more about diamonds, visit ABDO Publishing Company online. Web sites about diamonds are featured on our Book Links page. These links are routinely monitored and updated to provide the most current information available.

www.abdopublishing.com

INDEX